Regions in Europe

Since the 1960s, the revival of regionalist movements and pressures from within States to strengthen democracy have led to forms of institutional regionalisation in a number of European countries. Today the situation is very different and it is questionable whether regions in Europe exert any great influence on the politics, economy and society of Europe.

Regions in Europe explores the state of regional control in an increasingly integrated Europe. The contributors argue that the 1960s trends have vanished and that the predicted rise of increased political power at the regional level has been slow to materialise and fraught with paradox. In searching for reasons as to why this has happened this study explores regions in relation to European integration, globalisation, the nation state, local government, and comparative and national perspectives, finding that there have been many factors affecting the development of regions in Europe. Combining theory and case studies from many of the main players in Europe including: Germany, France, UK, Italy, Spain, the Netherlands and Belgium, this study concludes that European regions remain weak political actors in European governance.

Regions in Europe draws together political scientists, economists, sociologists and international relations specialists, to highlight why and how regions have not evolved into a formidable level of government in Europe and what, if any, future they have. It is essential reading for those interested in regionalism, politics, economy, nation states and social groups in the new Europe.

Patrick Le Galès is CNRS Senior Research Fellow at the Centre de Recherches Administratives et Politiques, University of Rennes, and Associate Professor at IEP Paris and IEP Rennes. **Christian Lequesne** is Senior Research Fellow at the Centre d'Etudes et de Recherches Internationales of the Fondation Nationale des Sciences Politiques, Paris, and Associate Professor at IEP, Paris, and College of Europe, Bruges.

European Public Policy Series

Edited by Jeremy Richardson
Department of Government, University of Essex

Also available in the series:

Regions in Europe

Edited by Patrick Le Galès and
Christian Lequesne

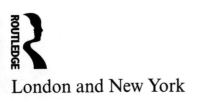

London and New York

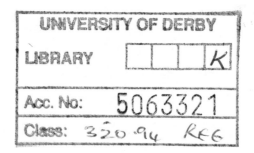
First published 1998
by Routledge
11 New Fetter Lane, London EC4P 4EE

Simultaneously published in the USA and Canada
by Routledge
29 West 35th Street, New York, NY 10001

Typeset in Times by Routledge
Printed and bound in Great Britain by Creative Print and Design
(Wales), Ebbw Vale

British Library Cataloguing in Publication Data
A catalogue record for this book is available from the British Library

Library of Congress Cataloguing in Publication Data
Le Galès, Patrick.
Regions in Europe/Patrick Le Galès and Christian Lequesne.
1. Regionalism – Europe, Western. I. Lequesne, Christian.
II. Title.
JN94.A38R4347   1998   97-26562
320.54`9`094–dc21   CIP

ISBN 0–415–16482–6 (hbk)
ISBN 0–415–16483–4 (pbk)